FLUTE FINGERING CHARTS
Scales & Songs

Kimber Books

ISBN: 978-1-969068-05-8
© 2025 The Martin Freres Company, Merimax, LLC
All Rights Reserved

Thank you!

Thank you for choosing Flute Fingering Charts, Scales and Songs. This book is designed for the Flute (Key of C) and serves as a clear, dependable reference for beginners and developing players.

Inside, you'll find fingering charts, scales, and familiar songs arranged to make learning both visual and musical. We begin with basic tutorials and gradually introduce more advanced concepts. Once you have the fundamentals down, you can jump to any section you like, and there is no required order.

Some scales and songs are easy and approachable, while others reach beyond the beginner flute range and may take more time to master. This book is meant to grow with you, serving as both an introduction and a lasting reference as your skills expand.

Each song includes a QR code that links directly to its audio recording. Listening before you play helps you understand how the notes fit together and strengthens your sense of tone, rhythm, and musical phrasing.

We hope this book becomes a steady companion on your musical journey, one you can return to often whether you're playing your first notes or exploring new challenges.

Happy playing!

Martin Freres

the
MARTIN FRERES COMPANY
MartinFreres.net

Let's Begin

Learning to play the flute can feel tricky at first, especially when trying to figure out which fingers to use for the notes on the page. That's why this book has fingering charts right below each note. These charts make it much easier to focus on playing instead of guessing. Here's how to use them.

Understand the Fingering Chart
Each note comes with a fingering diagram that shows you exactly which keys to press.
   - Black circles mean press this key down.
   - White and Gray circles mean don't press this key.

The fingering chart shown here is used for all the scales and songs in this book. On the music staff, the names of the notes are written above the staff to help you know what to play. Under each note, you'll see a fingering diagram that shows you where to put your fingers on the flute. This makes it easier to match the notes to the proper finger positions.

Notes to Play:
Letter above - Note below

Flute Fingering

For each note, press only the keys that are solid black.

By using the flute fingering charts, you'll learn faster and have more fun playing, now!

How to Use the QR Codes

Scan the QR code with your phone or tablet camera to hear the song. Listen and play what you hear. QR codes allow you to hear how the notes and rhythm sound together.

Scan the QR Code

to Listen!

Flute Fingering
Which Finger Goes Where?

Headjoint
(mouthpiece)

Embouchure Hole

Lip Plate

Body

Footjoint

THUMB

1

2

3

LEFT HAND ZONE

PINKY

1

1

2

2

3

RIGHT HAND ZONE

PINKY

Left Hand   Right Hand

1 = Index Finger
2 = Middle FInger
3 = Ring Finger
4 = Pinky Finger

TIP: Start with your left hand on top and your right hand on bottom.
Your left-hand thumb rests on the thumb key on the back.

How to Hold the Flute

1. Your Chin Is Your Main Anchor

Start by placing the embouchure hole to the center of you lips, then roll it outward so the lip plate rests beneath your bottom lip. Let the headjoint rest lightly against your chin. This is your main anchor and holds the flute steady without pressing down into it.

2. Your Left Hand Index Finger

Your left index finger holds the flute steady. The first knuckle rests lightly against the flute just under the key area. Its only job is to stop the flute from rolling. Keep the finger curved and relaxed so it can easily press key 1 for the left hand. Do not press or grip with it. Your finger is a gentle resting point.

3. Your Right Hand Thumb

Your right thumb supports the flute from below. Place it where it naturally lands when your right-hand fingers hover over the proper keys. Keep your thumb angled slightly upward so it lifts the flute rather than gripping it.

Holding the Flute

Your fingers should stay curved over the keys without tension. Only the fingers needed for the note press down. All others hover. When you play notes that use few fingers on the keys, hold the flute with the three support points. If the flute feels wobbly, check your three-point balance: lip plate on the chin, left index knuckle, and right thumb.

Hold the flute slightly downward to your right. Keep shoulders down, elbows natural, and arms relaxed. The headjoint stays steady while your fingers move freely. If you tilt or lift your arms to keep the flute stable, it means one of your support points needs adjusting.

Testing Your Balance

Place the flute lip plate on your chin. Position your left index knuckle. Position your right thumb. Remove all other fingers. If the flute stays balanced, your support is correct. If it rolls, one of the contact points is off.

Learning to Play the Flute

Making a Sound

Making a sound on the flute is one of the hardest parts for beginners. Start with just the headjoint (the mouthpiece). *Place the embouchure hole at the center of your lips.* Then roll the headjoint so the hole rolls away from your lips. Let your bottom lip rest on the lip plate, right at the edge of the hole. Leave a tiny space between your lips, like you're quietly saying "boo." Now blow gently across the hole, slightly downward. Once you can get a tone with just the headjoint, assemble the flute and try changing how hard you blow and the angle of your air until a clear, steady tone comes out. This takes practice, practice, practice.

Use the Charts While Learning Scales & Songs

When you start playing Scales & Songs, keep using the fingering charts as a guide. Play one note at a time and check your fingers if you need to. After a while, your fingers will begin to remember where to go, and you can follow the music sheet instead of the fingering charts.

Listen for Accuracy

Even if your fingers are in the right spots, your sound might still not be quite right if your breath control or lip positioning (embouchure) isn't right. Use the charts to make sure your fingers are correct, but also focus on creating a clear, steady sound for each note.

Move Away from the Charts

As you get better, challenge yourself to play scales and songs by looking only at the notes on the staff. Let your fingers do the work from memory. The more you practice this way, the more confident and independent you'll become.

Use the Charts When You Need Help

If you're struggling with a note or forgetting a fingering, don't worry, just look at the fingering charts. They're there to help you when you need a quick reminder.

By practicing with these charts and gradually using them less, you'll build strong skills faster and with less frustration. Always remember, the goal is not just to play notes, it's to make music. With time and effort, you'll be playing with confidence and having fun.

Starter C Major Scale

This is the starter C major scale beginning with the note A rather than C. This allows new players to learn a scale before reaching for lower or higher notes that can be tricky to learn. For this version, the notes are: A, B, C, D, E, F, G, then back to A.

For beginners, playing full scales can take time. Some of the lowest and highest notes need more practice, and that is perfectly fine. Play the notes you can, learn them at your own pace, and grow into the rest as you continue.

Each note comes with a fingering diagram showing you which keys to press.
   - Black circles mean press this key down.
   - White and Gray circles mean don't press this key.

Scan the QR Code

to Listen to the scale!

C Major Scale (Up)

Practicing the C major scale helps train your ear to hear the sound of a major key, which is important for playing songs and understanding how music fits together. We call it "Up" because the scale begins on the lower C note and moves higher with each new note. This scale is also known as the **C major scale ascending**, and it uses the notes C, D, E, F, G, A, and B. You will find these notes in many of the songs in this book.

For beginners, playing full scales can take time. Some of the lowest and highest notes need more practice, and that is perfectly fine. Play the notes you can, learn them at your own pace, and grow into the rest as you continue.

Many lower and higher notes on the flute use the same fingering. To reach the lower or higher sound, adjust your air by using a gentler, downward stream for low notes and a smaller, faster, more focused stream for high notes. Here, the lower C and higher C use the same fingering. Try it!

Each note comes with a fingering diagram showing you which keys to press.
- Black circles mean press this key down.
- White and Gray circles mean don't press this key.

Scan the QR Code

to Listen to the scale!

C Major Scale (Down)

Here is the C major scale going down. We call it "Down" because the scale begins on the higher C note and every new note goes lower in sound. This is also known as the **C major scale descending** and we will play the notes C, B, A, G, F, E, D, then back to C, only lower.

For beginners, playing full scales can take time. Some of the lowest and highest notes need more practice, and that is perfectly fine. Play the notes you can, learn them at your own pace, and grow into the rest as you continue.

Many lower and higher notes on the flute use the same fingering. To reach the lower or higher sound, adjust your air by using a gentler, downward stream for low notes and a smaller, faster, more focused stream for high notes. Here, the lower C and higher C use the same fingering. Try it!

Remember, each note comes with a fingering diagram showing you which keys to press.
- Black circles mean press this key down.
- White and Gray circles mean don't press this key.

Scan the QR Code

to Listen to the scale!

G Major Scale (Up)

This is the G major scale ascending. The scale begins on the G note and moves higher in sound with each new note. The G major scale includes the notes G, A, B, C, D, E, and F# (F sharp). The word **sharp** means the note sounds slightly higher in pitch than the regular note, in this case F.

For beginners, playing full scales can take time. Some of the lowest and highest notes need more practice, and that is perfectly fine. Play the notes you can, learn them at your own pace, and grow into the rest as you continue.

Many lower and higher notes on the flute use the same fingering. To reach the lower or higher sound, adjust your air by using a gentler, downward stream for low notes and a smaller, faster, more focused stream for high notes. Here, the lower G and higher G use the same fingering. Try it!

Remember, each note comes with a fingering diagram showing you which keys to press.
  - Black circles mean press this key down.
  - White and Gray circles mean don't press this key.

Scan the QR Code

to Listen to the scale!

G Major Scale (Down)

Here is the G major scale descending. The scale begins on the higher G note and every new note goes lower in sound. For the G major scale descending we will play the notes G, F#, E, D, C, B, A, then back to G, only lower.

For beginners, playing full scales can take time. Some of the lowest and highest notes need more practice, and that is perfectly fine. Play the notes you can, learn them at your own pace, and grow into the rest as you continue.

Many lower and higher notes on the flute use the same fingering. To reach the lower or higher sound, adjust your air by using a gentler, downward stream for low notes and a smaller, faster, more focused stream for high notes. Here, the lower G and higher G use the same fingering. Try it!

Remember, each note comes with a fingering diagram showing you which keys to press.
- Black circles mean press this key down.
- White and Gray circles mean don't press this key.

Scan the QR Code

to Listen to the scale!

F Major Scale (Up)

This is the F major scale ascending. The scale begins on the F note and moves higher in sound with each new note. The F major scale includes the notes F, G, A, B♭ (B flat), C, D, and E. The word **flat** means the note sounds slightly lower in pitch than the regular note, in this case B.

For beginners, playing full scales can take time. Some of the lowest and highest notes need more practice, and that is perfectly fine. Play the notes you can, learn them at your own pace, and grow into the rest as you continue.

Many lower and higher notes on the flute use the same fingering. To reach the lower or higher sound, adjust your air by using a gentler, downward stream for low notes and a smaller, faster, more focused stream for high notes. Here, the lower F and higher F use the same fingering. Try it!

Remember, each note comes with a fingering diagram showing you which keys to press.
- Black circles mean press this key down.
- White and Gray circles mean don't press this key.

Scan the QR Code

to Listen to the scale!

F Major Scale (Down)

Here is the F major scale descending. The scale begins on the higher F note and every new note goes lower in sound. For the F major scale descending we will play the notes F, E, D, C, B♭, A, G, then back to F, only lower.

For beginners, playing full scales can take time. Some of the lowest and highest notes need more practice, and that is perfectly fine. Play the notes you can, learn them at your own pace, and grow into the rest as you continue.

Many lower and higher notes on the flute use the same fingering. To reach the lower or higher sound, adjust your air by using a gentler, downward stream for low notes and a smaller, faster, more focused stream for high notes. Here, the lower F and higher F use the same fingering. Try it!

Remember, each note comes with a fingering diagram showing you which keys to press.
  - Black circles mean press this key down.
  - White and Gray circles mean don't press this key.

Scan the QR Code

to Listen to the scale!

D Major Scale (Up)

This is the D major scale ascending. The scale begins on the D note and moves higher in sound with each new note. The D major scale includes the notes D, E, F#, G, A, B, and C#.

For beginners, playing full scales can take time. Some of the lowest and highest notes need more practice, and that is perfectly fine. Play the notes you can, learn them at your own pace, and grow into the rest as you continue.

Many lower and higher notes on the flute use the same fingering. To reach the lower or higher sound, adjust your air by using a gentler, downward stream for low notes and a smaller, faster, more focused stream for high notes. Here, the lower D and higher D use the same fingering. Try it!

Remember, each note comes with a fingering diagram showing you which keys to press.
  - Black circles mean press this key down.
  - White and Gray circles mean don't press this key.

Scan the QR Code

to Listen to the scale!

D Major Scale (Down)

Here is the D major scale descending. The scale begins on the higher D note and every new note goes lower in sound. For the D major scale descending we will play the notes D, C#, B, A, G, F#, E, then back to D, only lower.

For beginners, playing full scales can take time. Some of the lowest and highest notes need more practice, and that is perfectly fine. Play the notes you can, learn them at your own pace, and grow into the rest as you continue.

Many lower and higher notes on the flute use the same fingering. To reach the lower or higher sound, adjust your air by using a gentler, downward stream for low notes and a smaller, faster, more focused stream for high notes. Here, the lower D and higher D use the same fingering. Try it!

Remember, each note comes with a fingering diagram showing you which keys to press.
   - Black circles mean press this key down.
   - White and Gray circles mean don't press this key.

Scan the QR Code

to Listen to the scale!

B♭ Major Scale (Up)

This is the B♭ major scale ascending. The scale begins on the B♭ note and moves higher in sound with each new note. The B♭ major scale includes the notes B♭, C, D, E♭, F, G, and A.

For beginners, playing full scales can take time. Some of the lowest and highest notes need more practice, and that is perfectly fine. Play the notes you can, learn them at your own pace, and grow into the rest as you continue.

Many lower and higher notes on the flute use the same fingering. To reach the lower or higher sound, adjust your air by using a gentler, downward stream for low notes and a smaller, faster, more focused stream for high notes. Here, the lower B♭ and higher B♭ use the same fingering. Try it!

Remember, each note comes with a fingering diagram showing you which keys to press.
- Black circles mean press this key down.
- White and Gray circles mean don't press this key.

Scan the QR Code

to Listen to the scale!

B♭ Major Scale (Down)

Here is the B♭ major scale descending. The scale begins on the higher B♭ note and every new note goes lower in sound. For the B♭ major scale descending we will play the notes B♭, A, G, F, E♭, D, C, then back to B♭, only lower.

For beginners, playing full scales can take time. Some of the lowest and highest notes need more practice, and that is perfectly fine. Play the notes you can, learn them at your own pace, and grow into the rest as you continue.

Many lower and higher notes on the flute use the same fingering. To reach the lower or higher sound, adjust your air by using a gentler, downward stream for low notes and a smaller, faster, more focused stream for high notes. Here, the lower B♭ and higher B♭ use the same fingering. Try it!

Remember, each note comes with a fingering diagram showing you which keys to press.
   - Black circles mean press this key down.
   - White and Gray circles mean don't press this key.

Scan the QR Code

to Listen to the scale!

E♭ Major Scale (Up)

This is the E♭ major scale ascending. The scale begins on the E♭ note and moves higher in sound with each new note. The E♭ major scale includes the notes E♭, F, G, A♭, B♭, C, and D.

For beginners, playing full scales can take time. Some of the lowest and highest notes need more practice, and that is perfectly fine. Play the notes you can, learn them at your own pace, and grow into the rest as you continue.

Many lower and higher notes on the flute use the same fingering. To reach the lower or higher sound, adjust your air by using a gentler, downward stream for low notes and a smaller, faster, more focused stream for high notes. Here, the lower E♭ and higher E♭ use the same fingering. Try it!

Remember, each note comes with a fingering diagram showing you which keys to press.
  - Black circles mean press this key down.
  - White and Gray circles mean don't press this key.

Scan the QR Code

to Listen to the scale!

Eb Major Scale (Down)

Here is the Eb major scale descending. The scale begins on the higher Eb note and every new note goes lower in sound. For the Eb major scale descending we will play the notes Eb, D, C, Bb, Ab, G, F, then back to Eb, only lower.

For beginners, playing full scales can take time. Some of the lowest and highest notes need more practice, and that is perfectly fine. Play the notes you can, learn them at your own pace, and grow into the rest as you continue.

Many lower and higher notes on the flute use the same fingering. To reach the lower or higher sound, adjust your air by using a gentler, downward stream for low notes and a smaller, faster, more focused stream for high notes. Here, the lower Eb and higher Eb use the same fingering. Try it!

Remember, each note comes with a fingering diagram showing you which keys to press.
- Black circles mean press this key down.
- White and Gray circles mean don't press this key.

Scan the QR Code

to Listen to the scale!

What is Your Embouchure?

em·bou·chure | \ ˌäm-bü-ˈshu̇r

Your flute embouchure is the way you shape your lips, mouth, and facial muscles to direct the airstream across the tone hole (embouchure hole). It's the main control point for your sound. The angle, firmness, and size of the lip opening all work together to create tone, pitch, and projection.

Small, gentle adjustments work best. Never force the sound. A balanced embouchure helps each note speak clearly and makes playing feel easier.

What Is Embouchure Pressure?
On the flute, "pressure" doesn't mean pushing or tightening. Instead, it refers to the gentle firmness of the lips and the focus of the air as it moves across the embouchure hole.

If the balance isn't quite right, the flute will tell you:

Too much tension
- Tone becomes tight or sharp
- Notes feel difficult to produce
- Air feels forced rather than flowing

Too little focus
- Sound becomes airy or unfocused
- Notes may not speak immediately
- Tone can feel wide or fuzzy

The goal is a relaxed lip shape with a steady, centered airstream that strikes the edge of the tone hole at the proper angle. Watching yourself in a mirror can help you see and adjust the shape and angle.

Tips to Improve Your Embouchure

Bottom Lip: Rest the lip plate lightly against the center of your bottom lip, covering a small part of the tone hole.

Top Lip: Shape the top lip to angle the air slightly downward. Keep it relaxed, not tight.

Lip Shape: Form a small, focused opening like saying "boo" to direct a steady, centered airstream.

Notes, Beats & How to Count Them

Here's a quick guide to the most common note types and how long each one lasts. In this book, we focus on learning to play by listening to the piece and then playing what you hear. You'll learn more about timing as you continue your musical journey.

Eighth (8th) notes
Each eighth note lasts for half a beat. Use steady air and move quickly to the next note.

When we see a plus sign: + we say 'and'

Quarter notes
A quarter note lasts 1 full beat. Use steady air and hold each note for one full beat. Each beat lasts the same amount of time.

Half notes
We play each half note for a count of 2 beats. Use steady air and hold each note for a full 2 beats. Each note lasts the same amount of time.

Whole notes
We count each whole note for 4 full beats. Use steady air and hold for 4 beats.

Dotted Quarter notes last for one and a half beats (that's 3 half beats).

How it works

A dot adds a little extra time—half the value of the note it's attached to.

Dotted Half notes each count for 3 beats. Use steady air and hold for 3 beats.

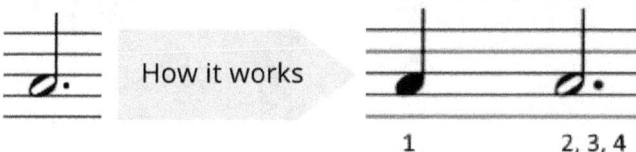

How it works

B Major Scale (Up)

This is the B major scale ascending. The scale begins on the B note and moves higher in sound with each new note. The B major scale includes the notes B, C#, D#, E, F#, G#, and A#.

For beginners, playing full scales can take time. Some of the lowest and highest notes need more practice, and that is perfectly fine. Play the notes you can, learn them at your own pace, and grow into the rest as you continue.

Many lower and higher notes on the flute use the same fingering. To reach the lower or higher sound, adjust your air by using a gentler, downward stream for low notes and a smaller, faster, more focused stream for high notes. Here, the lower B and higher B use the same fingering. Try it!

Remember, each note comes with a fingering diagram showing you which keys to press.
  - Black circles mean press this key down.
  - White and Gray circles mean don't press this key.

Scan the QR Code

to Listen to the scale!

B Major Scale (Down)

Here is the B major scale descending. The scale begins on the higher B note and every new note goes lower in sound. For the B major scale descending we will play the notes B, A#, G#, F#, E, D#, C#, then back to B, only lower.

For beginners, playing full scales can take time. Some of the lowest and highest notes need more practice, and that is perfectly fine. Play the notes you can, learn them at your own pace, and grow into the rest as you continue.

Many lower and higher notes on the flute use the same fingering. To reach the lower or higher sound, adjust your air by using a gentler, downward stream for low notes and a smaller, faster, more focused stream for high notes. Here, the lower B and higher B use the same fingering. Try it!

Remember, each note comes with a fingering diagram showing you which keys to press.
- Black circles mean press this key down.
- White and Gray circles mean don't press this key.

Scan the QR Code

to Listen to the scale!

E Major Scale (Up)

This is the E major scale ascending. The scale begins on the E note and moves higher in sound with each new note. The E major scale includes the notes E, F#, G#, A, B, C#, and D#.

For beginners, playing full scales can take time. Some of the lowest and highest notes need more practice, and that is perfectly fine. Play the notes you can, learn them at your own pace, and grow into the rest as you continue.

Many lower and higher notes on the flute use the same fingering. To reach the lower or higher sound, adjust your air by using a gentler, downward stream for low notes and a smaller, faster, more focused stream for high notes. Here, the lower E and higher E use the same fingering. Try it!

Remember, each note comes with a fingering diagram showing you which keys to press.
- Black circles mean press this key down.
- White and Gray circles mean don't press this key.

Scan the QR Code

to Listen to the scale!

E Major Scale (Down)

Here is the E major scale descending. The scale begins on the higher E note and every new note goes lower in sound. For the E major scale descending we will play the notes E, D#, C#, B, A, G#, F#, then back to E, only lower.

For beginners, playing full scales can take time. Some of the lowest and highest notes need more practice, and that is perfectly fine. Play the notes you can, learn them at your own pace, and grow into the rest as you continue.

Many lower and higher notes on the flute use the same fingering. To reach the lower or higher sound, adjust your air by using a gentler, downward stream for low notes and a smaller, faster, more focused stream for high notes. Here, the lower E and higher E use the same fingering. Try it!

Remember, each note comes with a fingering diagram showing you which keys to press.
   - Black circles mean press this key down.
   - White and Gray circles mean don't press this key.

Scan the QR Code

to Listen to the scale!

Db Major Scale (Up)

This is the Db major scale ascending. The scale begins on the Db note and moves higher in sound with each new note. The Db major scale includes the notes Db, Eb, F, Gb, Ab, Bb, and C.

For beginners, playing full scales can take time. Some of the lowest and highest notes need more practice, and that is perfectly fine. Play the notes you can, learn them at your own pace, and grow into the rest as you continue.

Notice that the higher and lower Db fingerings are not the same. Watch your flute balance on that high Db note using your chin, your left-hand index finger knuckle, and your right-hand thumb.

Remember, each note comes with a fingering diagram showing you which keys to press.
- Black circles mean press this key down.
- White and Gray circles mean don't press this key.

Scan the QR Code

to Listen to the scale!

Db Major Scale (Down)

Here is the Db major scale descending. The scale begins on the higher Db note and every new note goes lower in sound. For the Db major scale descending we will play the notes Db, C, Bb, Ab, Gb, F, Eb, then back to Db, only lower.

For beginners, playing full scales can take time. Some of the lowest and highest notes need more practice, and that is perfectly fine. Play the notes you can, learn them at your own pace, and grow into the rest as you continue.

Notice that the higher and lower Db fingerings are not the same. Watch your flute balance on that high Db note using your chin, your left-hand index finger knuckle, and your right-hand thumb.

Remember, each note comes with a fingering diagram showing you which keys to press.
 - Black circles mean press this key down.
 - White and Gray circles mean don't press this key.

Scan the QR Code

to Listen to the scale!

A♭ Major Scale (Up)

This is the A♭ major scale ascending. The scale begins on the A♭ note and moves higher in sound with each new note. The A♭ major scale includes the notes A♭, B♭, C, D♭, E♭, F, and G.

For beginners, playing full scales can take time. Some of the lowest and highest notes need more practice, and that is perfectly fine. Play the notes you can, learn them at your own pace, and grow into the rest as you continue.

Many lower and higher notes on the flute use the same fingering. To reach the lower or higher sound, adjust your air by using a gentler, downward stream for low notes and a smaller, faster, more focused stream for high notes. Here, the lower A♭ and higher A♭ use the same fingering. Try it!

Remember, each note comes with a fingering diagram showing you which keys to press.
   - Black circles mean press this key down.
   - White and Gray circles mean don't press this key.

Scan the QR Code

to Listen to the scale!

A♭ Major Scale (Down)

Here is the A♭ major scale descending. The scale begins on the higher A♭ note and every new note goes lower in sound. For the A♭ major scale descending we will play the notes A♭, G, F, E♭, D♭, C, B♭, then back to A♭, only lower.

For beginners, playing full scales can take time. Some of the lowest and highest notes need more practice, and that is perfectly fine. Play the notes you can, learn them at your own pace, and grow into the rest as you continue.

Many lower and higher notes on the flute use the same fingering. To reach the lower or higher sound, adjust your air by using a gentler, downward stream for low notes and a smaller, faster, more focused stream for high notes. Here, the lower A♭ and higher A♭ use the same fingering. Try it!

Remember, each note comes with a fingering diagram showing you which keys to press.
- Black circles mean press this key down.
- White and Gray circles mean don't press this key.

Scan the
QR Code

to Listen to
the scale!

A Major Scale (Up)

This is the A major scale ascending. The scale begins on the A note and moves higher in sound with each new note. The A major scale includes the notes A, B, C#, D, E, F#, and G#.

For beginners, playing full scales can take time. Some of the lowest and highest notes need more practice, and that is perfectly fine. Play the notes you can, learn them at your own pace, and grow into the rest as you continue.

Many lower and higher notes on the flute use the same fingering. To reach the lower or higher sound, adjust your air by using a gentler, downward stream for low notes and a smaller, faster, more focused stream for high notes. Here, the lower A and higher A use the same fingering. Try it!

Remember, each note comes with a fingering diagram showing you which keys to press.
- Black circles mean press this key down.
- White and Gray circles mean don't press this key.

Scan the QR Code

to Listen to the scale!

A Major Scale (Down)

Here is the A major scale descending. The scale begins on the higher A note and every new note goes lower in sound. For the A major scale descending we will play the notes A, G#, F#, E, D, C#, B, then back to A, only lower.

For beginners, playing full scales can take time. Some of the lowest and highest notes need more practice, and that is perfectly fine. Play the notes you can, learn them at your own pace, and grow into the rest as you continue.

Many lower and higher notes on the flute use the same fingering. To reach the lower or higher sound, adjust your air by using a gentler, downward stream for low notes and a smaller, faster, more focused stream for high notes. Here, the lower A and higher A use the same fingering. Try it!

Remember, each note comes with a fingering diagram showing you which keys to press.
   - Black circles mean press this key down.
   - White and Gray circles mean don't press this key.

Scan the QR Code

to Listen to the scale!

G♭ Major Scale (Up)

This is the G♭ major scale ascending. The scale begins on the G♭ note and moves higher in sound with each new note. The G♭ major scale includes the notes G♭, A♭, B♭, C♭ (C♭ is the same as B), D♭, E♭, and F.

In music, some notes can have two different names even though they sound exactly the same. This is called being enharmonic. C♭ (C flat) and B are one of these pairs.

When you see C♭, it means play one half step lower than C. When you move one half step lower from C, you land on B. So even though they look different on paper, C♭ and B sound the same when you play them.

Remember, each note comes with a fingering diagram showing you which keys to press.
- Black circles mean press this key down.
- White and Gray circles mean don't press this key.

Scan the QR Code

to Listen to the scale!

G♭ Major Scale (Down)

Here is the G♭ major scale descending. The scale begins on the higher G♭ note and every new note goes lower in sound. For the G♭ major scale descending we will play the notes G♭, F, E♭, D♭, C♭ (B), B♭, A♭, then back to G♭, only lower.

For beginners, playing full scales can take time. Some of the lowest and highest notes need more practice, and that is perfectly fine. Play the notes you can, learn them at your own pace, and grow into the rest as you continue.

Many lower and higher notes on the flute use the same fingering. To reach the lower or higher sound, adjust your air by using a gentler, downward stream for low notes and a smaller, faster, more focused stream for high notes. Here, the lower G♭ and higher G♭ use the same fingering. Try it!

Remember, each note comes with a fingering diagram showing you which keys to press.
- Black circles mean press this key down.
- White and Gray circles mean don't press this key.

Scan the QR Code

to Listen to the scale!

Mary Had a Little Lamb

Lowell Mason (1831)

The Legend of Mary and Her Lamb

As the legend goes, this song was inspired by an actual event involving a girl named Mary Elizabeth Sawyer (1806–1889), who lived in Sterling, Massachusetts. According to Mary's writings, when she was a young girl, she nursed a sickly lamb back to health, and the lamb became attached to her. One day, the lamb followed Mary to school, creating a scene that amused her classmates and teacher.

Today, the Redstone Schoolhouse, where Mary's lamb supposedly followed her, is preserved as a historical site in Sudbury, Massachusetts, and continues to commemorate the tale.

Scan the
QR Code

to Listen to
the song!

Twinkle Twinkle Little Star

Traditional (1806)

Scan the
QR Code

to Listen to
the song!

Frère Jacques (Brother John)

Traditional French (18th Century)

Scan the QR Code to Listen to the song!

Pop Goes the Weasel

Traditional English (c1850)

Scan the QR Code

to Listen to the song!

Ring Around the Rosie

Traditional English (19th Century)

Scan the QR Code

to Listen to the song!

Row Row Row Your Boat

Traditional American (19th Century)

Scan the
QR Code

to Listen to
the song!

This Old Man

Traditional English (19th Century)

Scan the QR Code to Listen to the song!

London Bridge is Falling Down

Traditional English (18th Century)

It's a Jazzy Day!

Martin Freres (2025)

It's a Jazzy Day!

This tune plays low notes and then jumps an octave higher. An **octave** is when a note is played again at a higher or lower pitch, but is still the same note. In this song, that happens with the lower and higher A note.

Scan the
QR Code

to Listen to
the song!

Camptown Races

Stephen Foster (1850)

Stephen C. Foster (1826–1864)

Known as the "Father of American Music," Stephen Foster wrote songs that became part of America's cultural history. Born in Pennsylvania on July 4, 1826, he composed beloved tunes such as *Camptown Races, Oh! Susanna,* and *That's What's the Matter*, all featured in this book. His music remains timeless, simple, and memorable, ideal for learning melody, rhythm, and phrasing.

Scan the QR Code

to Listen to the song!

Oh! Susanna

Stephen Foster (1848)

That's What's the Matter

Stephen Foster (1862)

Scan the QR Code

to Listen to the song!

Ode to Joy

Ludwig van Beethoven (1824)

She'll Be Comin' 'Round the Mountain

Traditional American (19th Century)

Scan the QR Code

to Listen to the song!

When the Saints Go Marching In

Traditional American (19th Century)

Scan the QR Code to Listen to the song!

Amazing Grace

William Walker (1835)

Musical History of "Amazing Grace"

The tune we use for *Amazing Grace* is an early American melody called *New Britain*. It's an old American melody that first appeared in a music book in 1829.

In 1835, a musician named William Walker arranged the *Amazing Grace* words with the *New Britain* melody in his book *Southern Harmony*. The two fit so well that the pairing quickly became popular all over the world. The rest is history!

Scan the QR Code

to Listen to the song!

Jingle Bells

J. Pierpont (1857)

Scan the QR Code to Listen to the song!

Up On the Housetop

Benjamin Hanby (1864)

Flute Fingering Chart

The Flute fingering chart begins with the note C4. Next, the chart rises step by step, showing flats (♭) and sharps (#), all the way up to C7. This fingering chart is presented as a chromatic scale.

A **Chromatic Scale** is a musical scale that goes up or down by half steps, the smallest steps in music. Think of playing every single note in order, without skipping any. Scan the QR code to listen to the whole scale from C4 to C7.

C4 to B4

Flute Fingering Chart

The numbers next to the notes, like 4, 5, and 6, are called octave numbers. Octave numbers are the numbers you see next to a note name, like C4 or F5. They tell you how high or low a note sounds on your instrument or in music. Each time you go from one C note to the next higher sounding C note, you move up one octave and the number increases by one. So, the number helps show which version of the note you're playing: low, middle, or high.

C5 to B5

Flute Fingering Chart

C6 to C7

Scan the QR Code to Listen to the scale!

History of the Flute

The flute is one of the oldest musical instruments in the world. The earliest flutes discovered were made from bird bones and mammoth ivory more than 40,000 years ago. These early instruments had a few holes and were blown across the edge, much like today's flute. Archaeologists found bone and ivory flutes in German caves that were radiocarbon-dated to 40,000–42,000 years old.

As civilizations grew, many cultures developed their own versions. Ancient Egyptians, Greeks, Chinese, and Native American cultures all created flutes, usually from wood, bone, or reed. In medieval Europe, a simple wooden flute called the "fife" was common.

During the Renaissance, flutes were made in one long piece of wood with six finger holes and no keys. These instruments could only play comfortably in a few keys.

Everything changed in the Baroque period thanks to Jacques-Martin Hotteterre (1674–1763), a French flutist and maker. Hotteterre redesigned the flute into three separate sections (headjoint, body, and footjoint), which improved tuning and made it easier to build more advanced versions. He also added the first key to the flute, expanding the range of notes and allowing better intonation. His design became the foundation for all future wooden flutes.

The next major leap came in the mid-1800s with Theobald Boehm, a German flutist, engineer, and instrument maker. Boehm redesigned the flute's entire mechanism. He replaced the old key system with a ring-key and rod mechanism, enlarged and repositioned the tone holes, and introduced metal tubing. His innovations created the modern concert flute used today in orchestras and bands.

From ancient bone instruments to Hotteterre's three-piece wooden flutes to Boehm's elegant metal design, the flute has evolved over thousands of years into a versatile, expressive instrument played in orchestras, bands, jazz groups, folk ensembles, and classrooms around the world.

Did You Know?
Most woodwinds use a reed, but some do not. Instruments like the flute, piccolo, and recorder make sound by blowing air across or into a hole.

Martin Freres
Paris LaMonte
Model 1 Flute
1940s

www.ingramcontent.com/pod-product-compliance
Lightning Source LLC
LaVergne TN
LVHW081336060426
835513LV00014B/1312